9780852630112

Discovering
COINS

George Berry

Photographs by G. V. G. Hill

Shire Publications, Tring, Herts.

CONTENTS

SBN 85263011 5

INTRODUCTION

Of recent years coins have caught the imagination of the public. We are beginning to look closely at the change in our pockets, and to take a keen interest in the designs of current coins. Undoubtedly this interest has been stimulated by the imminence of decimalisation, by the growing realisation that even modern coins in extremely fine condition may be a good investment, and by the tremendous growth in the number of coin dealers.

This booklet is an attempt to encourage readers not only to examine their coins more closely but to delve rather more deeply into the fascinating history that lies behind their minting, a history that spans a thousand years. It is not written specifically for the collector, but suggestions are given as to how ancient and medieval as well as modern coins may be collected at reasonable cost in these days of inflation. Coins are historical documents and invaluable tools for the historian and the teacher of history.

The writer, a lecturer in education, is amazed at how rarely coins are used in the teaching of history, especially in junior schools. Where children have been encouraged to look at coins, both ancient and modern, to handle them (in the correct way—by the edge!), to decipher the legends, to make discoveries about the kings and moneyers who struck them and the ordinary folk who used them and sometimes hoarded them, their insight into the processes of history has been far keeeener than that of children who have been nurtured entirely on books.

Few who embark on a discovery of coins, young and old alike, fail to succumb to its fascination, and become enthusiasts for life.

MINTS AND MINTING

The development of coining techniques in Britain

The earliest coins to be current in these islands appeared in the first century B.C. They were Celtic gold coins, bore no legend, and may well have been minted in Gaul. The first native coins to be manufactured here comprised the so-called Tin Money (100-75 B.C.). It is thought that wooden models were pressed into clay moulds, and that the coins were cast in strips. The first gold coinage struck in Britain appeared in north Kent about 70 B.C. Eventually the Iron Age Britons struck coins in gold, silver and bronze throughout Britain, normally between dies. The later bronze coinage of the Durotriges, who occupied the West Country, was cast in clay moulds. Existing coins were pressed into the mould as patterns. It is not surprising that the series showed a rapid deterioration.

During the early Roman occupation of Britain there is no evidence of official British mints, although many contemporary forgeries were made, particularly of the large bronze coins of Claudius. The majority were cast from authentic coins, but some were struck from the crudest of dies! Official British mints operated for a period of fifty years (A.D. 287-337). Only one is definitely known — London. The other was probably Colchester. Both mints were fortunate in their craftsmen who produced good quality coins. Little is known of Roman coin dies, and no official ones have survived.

The dies of early Anglo-Saxon coins were engraved by free hand, but in the ninth century the practice was adopted of forming the design with individual punches. These punches resembled minute chisels, and were used for building up the head of the monarch, the lettering of the legend and any other required design or pattern such as an ornamental cross. A separate punch was used for each dot, crescent or letter. One punch might have several uses. A pellet for example would represent either a stop in the legend, a pearl in the crown, an eye or the knob at the end of a sceptre.

A brief description of the minting process might be helpful at this stage. A pair of dies was necessary — one to bear the design of the obverse (or head) of the coin, the other the reverse (or tail) design. The dies were made of wrought iron. The lower die, known as the standard or pile, was pointed at one end so that it could be driven into a block of wood. The upper die called a trussel or puncheon was thicker and heavier as it had to bear the brunt of the heavy blows of the hammer. The designs were engraved by making punches on the smooth faces of the dies by die sinkers. The standard or pile carried the obverse design which was normally more difficult to engrave than the reverse. The reason underlying this procedure was that the standard normally lasted twice or three times as long as the trussel. In consequence a set of dies consisted of one standard or pile and two or even three trussels. It has been estimated that such a set could produce up to 20,000 coins.

When the dies had been made, the blanks would be prepared. The silver ore was melted in a crucible over a charcoal fire, cooled and then beaten on an anvil to a plate of required thickness. The plate was then cut into round "blanks" with a pair of shears and the blanks were trimmed. The blanks were placed individually between the dies and struck several times with the hammer. Some of the finished coins had to be put on one side so that they could be assayed before a jury to ensure that the coinage was of correct fineness and weight.

Inevitably in such a primitive method, imperfections occurred, such as mis-strikes and brockages. A mis-strike is a term used for a coin that has not been struck centrally due to the shifting of the die. The term double striking is often used for this fault. Sometimes a coin jammed in the die, unnoticed by the moneyer, and succeeding coins were consequently struck on one side only, normally the reverse. These are referred to as brockages.

In the year 1279 the minute punches, each containing a pellet, crescent or line, were replaced by slightly more comprehensive punches, each of which embraced a portion of the design. Although after the Middle Ages more and more of the design came to be transferred to a single large master punch, it was not until 1878 that this was completely achieved.

The introduction of machines in coin manufacture was a major innovation in minting history. Machinery was first used at the Paris Mint in 1552, and although some "milled" coins were produced at the London mint by a French engraver, Mestrell, during the years 1561-1571 in Elizabeth I's reign, the hammered method was not finally abandoned until 1662. The term "milled" does not refer to the grained edge of modern coins, but rather to the rolls of a mill powered by water or horses used in a reduction process.

Mestrell probably used a primitive screw press for his coinage. Another countryman of his, Nicholas Briot, mint engraver for Charles I, employed the screw press for small coins and the rocker press for half crowns and crowns. The screw press was operated by teams of four men, and up to 20 or 30 coins a minute could be struck by this method but at a cost of many strained muscles and severed fingers. The rocker press was so-called because the dies rocked against each other. The chief defect of the rocker press was that as oval cutters were used to produce the blocks, which became circular in passing between the dies, distortions frequently occurred, and many of the freshly minted coins were bowed and even buckled. Such presses were used at Aberystwyth, Oxford and Bristol, and perhaps even at the Tower mint itself.

The screw press, however, was permanently adopted at the mint for the production of all English coins in 1662. In the early nineteenth century, Boulton and Watt devised steam driven engines to operate the screw press, and the entire process of coining became more automatic. An entirely new building was erected on Tower Hill to accommodate this machinery, and it was opened in 1813. Further improvements followed embracing the introduction of reducing machinery in 1824, and the use of electricity in 1905. The following figures demonstrate the dramatic and continuous improvements and developments in techniques over the past hundred years.

Year	No. of coins produced per annum
1860	25 million
1890	70 million
1900	130 million
1920	260 million
1960	700 million

The imminent removal of the Royal Mint to South Wales opens up a new chapter in a fascinating history.

The distribution and centralisation of English mints

The settlement of the Angles and Saxons in these islands witnessed the establishment of a variety of regional mints. Each king issued money from his capital. At first the name of the mint did not appear on the coin. But as the kingdoms increased in size by conquest and several mints came under the control of a single monarch, it became common practice to put the mint name as well as that of the money on the coinage. The name of London first appears on coins about the year 825 when Mercia was conquered by Wessex and that of Canterbury a little earlier when Mercia gained control over Kent. It is interesting to note that the Archbishops of

Canterbury and York issued their own coinage in the eighth and ninth centuries. Undoubtedly this privilege was accorded by the Crown.

From the time of Alfred, London became the most important and most prolific mint. Alfred's London pennies, bearing his portrait and the London monogram, were issued in large numbers. After 900 London replaced Canterbury as the premier die cutting centre. The number of mints increased rapidly from 28 in Aethelstan's reign to between sixty and seventy in the reign of Edward the Confessor. Aethelstan actually stated the exact number of moneyers who should operate at each mint e.g. London: eight, Canterbury: seven, Winchester: six.

The possession of a mint is undoubtedly one of the acid tests of borough status, linking Watchet and Winchester, Cadbury (for a brief moment) and Canterbury. There are problems, however, as H. R. Loyn points out. Numerous sizeable Saxon boroughs such as Droitwich and Grantham have not so far yielded Saxon coins bearing their name. At the other extreme small villages such as Horndon in Essex, which issued coins in Edward the Confessor's reign, failed to develop into permanent boroughs.

The London mint remained the most prolific Saxon mint, producing a quarter of the country's output and was followed in order of importance by York (with about a tenth), Lincoln, Winchester, Chester, Norwich, Exeter and Thetford.

The Norman Conquest had no immediate effect on the Saxon pattern of minting. The Saxon moneyers were permitted to carry on with their work as before. The designs continued to be changed every two or three years, and sixty mints operated during William the Conqueror's reign.

Yet in line with a royal policy of increasing centralisation, the number of mints steadily decreased in the next two centuries, as the following figures show.

Coinage		No. of mints
William I and II	1066-1100	70
Henry I	1100-1135	53
Longcross	1180-1247	21
Shortcross	1247-1279	20
Edward I	1279-1307	12

By the fourteenth century minting became centralised in the Tower mint, although episcopal issues occurred spasmodically at Canterbury, York and Durham. Henry VIII not surprisingly suppressed the latter ecclesiastical mint, but supplemented the Tower mint production by using mints at Southwark, Canterbury, York and Bristol. These were eventually closed by Edward VI, and with the exception of two periods only, all gold and silver coins in England have been struck at the London mint. The Civil War saw the temporary establishment of mints at York, Aberystwyth, Combe Martin, Shrewsbury, Oxford and numerous other places and the great recoinage of William III in 1696 demanded the temporary use of mints at Bristol, Exeter, Chester, Norwich, and York.

Copper and bronze coins also have been struck at London in the main right up to the present day. The Soho Mint, Birmingham however, took over the copper coinage of George III from 1797 to 1807, whilst during the years 1874-6, 1881-2, 1912, 1918 and 1919 private mints in Birmingham issued a proportion of bronze pennies.

BRIEF HISTORIES OF ENGLISH COINS

The Penny

The first English pennies were made of silver, and were issued probably at Canterbury by a Saxon king of Kent, Aethelbert II (748-762). They replaced the smaller thicker sceats which circulated in many parts of early Saxon England, particularly in Northumbria and the south. The expression 'Scot free' is derived from the Saxon sceat.

The new pennies were copied from contemporary Frankish coins known as deniers, which took their name from the Roman silver coin, the *denarius* — hence the 'd' of £ — s. — d. They bore Aethelbert's portrait, facing right on the obverse (that is the 'head'), together with his name and that of the striker Lul. The reverse (or tail) showed a design of the wolf and twins, taken from a Roman coin of Constantine the Great. It was common practice in Saxon and Norman England for the moneyer to strike his own name on the coin as an additional guarantee.

The penny quickly established itself as the standard unit of currency. For almost five hundred years it was the only coin struck by English mints and for a thousand years (760-1797) it remained a silver coin. The Saxon penny originally weighed 22½ grains. There were 240 to the Saxon pound weight of silver.

Many Saxon pennies were of great beauty. Those of the great king of Mercia, Offa (757-796), were particularly pleasing. The designs were well executed, the standard of portraiture being unsurpassed. Alfred the Great (871-900) issued a wide variety of silver pennies, some with a portrait

8

and some without. Probably the most well known are the London pennies, which bear the king's portrait on the obverse and a monogram of London on the reverse.

As we might expect, more pennies of Aethelred II "the Unready" (976-1016) are dug up in Scandinavia than in England, having crossed the North Sea as danegeld to buy off the Viking invaders. No less than sixty mints operated in his reign. The long cross is beginning to appear regularly on the reverse of coins as a standard feature, facilitating the cutting of half pennies and quarter pennies (farthings). The later Saxon kings changed the designs on their pennies every few years in order to gain increased revenue. Edward the Confessor for example had ten main types. When a new type was produced coins of previous issues were called in and melted down. Thus Saxon and Norman hoards do not usually contain a wide variety of types.

The Norman conquest had little immediate effect on the evolution of the penny. Its weight, design and method of minting remained as before, since William realised that English pennies were of a better quality than Norman. During the reigns of William Rufus, Henry I and Stephen the penny became increasingly poorly struck. By the beginning of the reign of Henry II it was extremely degraded. It was severely misshapen and its inscription was barely legible. This first issue of Henry II pence was known as the Tealby coinage after the famous Tealby hoard of 1807.

Towards the end of Henry II's reign in 1180, however, a new series of pence was instituted, referred to nowadays as the shortcross coinage because of the reverse design. A goldsmith from Anjou named Philip Aimery was responsible for the new design. The first shortcross pennies of Henry II were a great improvement on the Tealby coinage. Unfortunately the standard of workmanship deteriorated during the reigns of his sons, Richard Coeur de Lion and John. During this century clipping was practised on a large scale. Dishonest persons would shave off the edge of their coins with a pair of shears, and melt down the silver shavings. Many of the coins of this period that you will see are misshapen as a result of this practice. In order to prevent such an abuse, in 1247 new longcross pennies were issued, the short cross on the reverse being extended to the edge of the coin. The longcross coinage lasted until 1279. Clipping still continued however, the Jews being held chiefly responsible, as the following extract from *A Chronicle of London* (1278) shows:

"the VIII day of seynt Martyn, all the Jewes of England were taken for clippying of money."

It is significant that the Jews were expelled from the country in 1290.

The new pence of Edward I (1279) were much improved in design and workmanship, and became the model for the next two hundred years. They were no longer the sole denomination, for groats, half pennies and farthings were issued too. Although Saxon and Norman pennies are becoming scarce and expensive, some types of shortcross, longcross and Edward pennies are common and may be obtained for a pound or thirty shillings each. They are so common because of the several hoards containing thousands that have been discovered. Pennies continued to be issued throughout medieval and Tudor times, but they became smaller in size and less significant. The groat valued at fourpence became a more popular coin.

The first copper penny appeared in 1797 during the reign of George III. It was a heavy coin weighing 1 oz. and was produced at the Soho Mint, Birmingham by Matthew Boulton. At the same time a 2 oz. two penny piece was minted, the heaviest English coin ever produced. Both were nicknamed 'cartwheels' because of their heavy rims. Boulton intended to use his new coinage as part of an integrated system of money, weights and measures. Thus eight two penny pieces weighed 1 lb. and measured 1 foot. 16 penny pieces weighed 1 lb. and 17 measured 2 feet.

The cartwheel pennies were unpopular because of their inconvenient size and weight, and were replaced in 1799 by smaller copper pennies. The first type of Victorian pennies bearing the "young head" portrait of the Queen designed by William Wyon, were of copper, and were larger and heavier than our present bronze pennies. The year 1860 is a significant one in the history of the penny. In that year it was reduced to its present size, more convenient for handling, and bronze replaced copper. Only bronze coins issued in or after 1860 are acceptable today as legal tender.

The new coins were nicknamed "bun" pennies, because the Queen's hair was coiled in a bun. The design, this time by Leonard Wyon, proved extremely popular probably because the Queen appeared so youthful. "Bun" pennies, depicting the Queen in her thirties, were still being issued in 1894, when the Queen was seventy four! During the years 1874-6 and 1881-2 the Birmingham mint of Ralph Heaton and Sons was asked to supplement the bronze coins issued by the London mint. You can detect the Heaton coins by looking for a small h below the date.

Thomas Brock's "old head" design graced the bronze

coinage during the last six years of Queen Victoria's reign. They were minted in large numbers and are extremely common. No pennies were issued for circulation in the years 1923-25, 1933, 1941-43, 1952, 1954-60. The largest number of pennies issued in a single year was in 1936 when 134,160,000 were minted. Low mintage years for pennies were 1950 (240,000), 1951 (120,000) and 1953 (1,308,647). Pennies of these years in Extremely Fine condition are in great demand. You may have heard of the legendary pennies of 1933. Only six of that year were thought to be minted. Three rest safely in museum cabinets, two lie under foundation stones of Yorkshire churches and a sixth lies beneath the university buildings in London. Two more have, however, recently come to light!

The Half Penny

Before the reign of Edward I, half pennies were literally pennies cut in half. The cross design on the reverse of Saxon and Norman pennies enabled the moneyer to cut half pennies and fourthlings or farthings with ease. There had been a few round half pennies at the time of Alfred, but they had not proved popular. The year 1280 saw the general adoption of the round half penny. This was a silver coin like the penny. The half penny remained of silver until Charles II's reign. In 1672 copper half pennies were struck bearing on the reverse the figure of Britannia. This device was adopted from the Roman coinage of Hadrian and Antoninus Pius. As Samuel Pepys tells us in his *Diary* 25th February 1667, Charles' favourite cousin, Frances Stewart, later Duchess of Richmond, provided the inspiration for this seventeenth century Britannia. Tin half pennies were struck for a short period, but this practice was abandoned in 1694. After 1860 half pennies like pennies and farthings were struck in bronze. In 1937, Britannia was replaced by the present sailing vessel inspired by Drake's *Golden Hind* which sailed round the world. The most uncommon half penny in circulation is that of 1871.

The Farthing

The first farthings consisted of pennies cut into four. Saxon and Norman hoards frequently contain specimens of these fragments. Edward I introduced the first round farthings of silver in 1280. They continued to be issued until the reign of Edward VI but were never very common or popular on account of their minute size. The reluctance of the mint in Tudor times to replace them with coins of a baser metal led to a scarcity of small change. Quite naturally traders began to issue lead or pewter tokens of their own, valued at a

11

half penny or farthing. James I put a stop to this practice by authorising Lord Harrington to strike copper farthing tokens privately but in the king's name. The Harrington farthings bear the royal legend together with a crown and crossed sceptres. An Irish harp adorns the reverse. They possessed mint marks just like official coinage. Unfortunately they were treated with some suspicion, and twenty one shillings worth had to be accumulated before a pounds worth of silver coinage could be obtained in exchange. They were also extensively forged. The patent passed on in turn to the Duke of Lennox, his widow, the Duchess of Richmond and Lord Maltravers. The later Maltravers farthings bear a crowned rose on the reverse. They were rather smaller than their predecessors, and some were plugged to discourage forgery.

The first official copper farthings were struck in 1672 by order of Charles II. They bore the same design as the half penny. Twelve years later an experimental issue was made of tin farthings as an economic measure. They bore the rather apologetic inscription *NUMMORUM FAMULUS* — the servant of coins. In 1694, however, the experiment was abandoned. The new copper farthings were made of English rather than Swedish ore, as previously.

The 1714 farthing of Queen Anne is particularly interesting. The Queen herself provided the model for Britannia. With regal decorum even the ankles are covered! Hitherto one leg had been bared to the knee. Cartwheel farthings were issued at Soho, Birmingham in 1799, 1806 and 1807. In 1897 the mint issued farthings of a particularly dark finish in order to prevent confusion between the farthing and the gold half sovereign. This practice continued until 1915 when half sovereigns were discontinued.

Britannia remained on the farthing until 1937 when she was replaced by the wren designed by Wilson Parker. The farthing was finally withdrawn from circulation in 1956.

Half farthings originally struck for use in Ceylon were proclaimed official currency in 1842, but they were little more than curiosities, and were discontinued in 1856.

A milled silver coin of three farthings was struck during the reign of Elizabeth I but this is now extremely rare. Shakespeare referred to the profile and the rose by the Queen's head in his play *King John*:

My face so thin
That in my ear I durst not stick a rose
Lest men should say, look where three farthings goes.

12

The Three Pence

The threepenny piece made its debut alongside the sixpence in 1551 as part of the recoinage of Edward VI. At first there was little justification for its existence as groats and half groats valued at four pence and two pence respectively were already in circulation. Elizabeth I, however, suspended the minting of half groats for sixteen years to enable the three-pence to establish itself. Despite this help, no further threepenny pieces were struck until the Civil War. The coin disappeared again by the eighteenth century except as a Maundy piece.

Maundy money consists of four small silver coins ranging from a penny to fourpence. Originally current coins of the realm were used for the Maundy ceremony. During the eighteenth century it became customary for special Maundy money to be issued. The ceremony is derived from the washing of the Disciples' feet after the Last Supper on the evening prior to the Crucifixion and normally takes place in Westminster Abbey on Maundy Thursday (the day before Good Friday). The number of pence contained in the purse corresponded to the age of the monarch.

In 1845 large numbers of three penny pieces bearing the same design as the Maundy threepence of that year were put into circulation. They became so popular that the days of the groat (fourpence) were numbered. The groat in fact disappeared in 1855.

The silver three penny piece so popular in the Victorian era became heavily criticised in the twentieth century for its small size. The year 1937 marked the appearance of the dumpy nickel brass dodecagonal (twelve-sided) three penny bit. It was so successful a substitute that the silver coin disappeared altogether in 1945. The reverse design of the original threepence bore a clump of thrift or sea pink from a drawing by Miss Madge Kitchener. The portcullis design of the present threepence was modelled by Mr. W. Gardner.

The Groat

The groat, next to the penny, was the coin most universally used in later medieval England. Its name suggests great or thick coin, and like the French *gros* or German *groschen* was derived from the *grossi denari* struck in Bohemia at the beginning of the fourteenth century.

The English groat copied the French *gros Tournois,* a billon piece of four deniers struck originally at the Abbey of St. Martin at Tours. (Billon is an alloy of copper and silver.) Edward I added the groat to the English coinage in 1279.

Hitherto the penny had been the only denomination in circulation. The design of the new groat was original and pleasing, consisting of a facing portrait crowned within a quatrefoil on the obverse and a long cross fleury on the reverse. New royal titles appear on the legend — Duke of Aquitaine and Lord of Ireland. The population at this period must have been too traditional and conservative in its habits, however, for it refused to accept the groat which did not reappear until 1351. Shortly after this date an "English" mint was established at Calais, and groats together with other coinage were minted there until the reign of Henry VI (1422-71). The Calais groats bear the words *VILLA CALESIE* on the reverse. From 1400 onwards it became common practice for privy marks to appear on coins. These took various forms such as an unusual initial cross, a deliberate misspelling, a peculiar stop, an extra anulet on the obverse. These marks changed every three months and seem to indicate the moneyer responsible for striking the various issues.

Particularly handsome portrait groats of Henry VII and Henry VIII were produced. The groats of the third coinage of Henry VIII, however, showing his older, bearded full face were considerably debased. Groats remained current until 1662.

A much smaller silver piece valued at fourpence now known as the Britannia groat was struck during the reigns of William IV and Queen Victoria, but these were finally discontinued in 1855, being replaced by the silver threepence. The name Britannia groat is self explanatory. When they were issued they were nicknamed in derision "fourpenny joeys" by cabbies, after the politician, Joseph Hume, who urged the use of the fourpenny piece to pay short cab fares rather than the sixpence.

The Sixpence

Edward VI launched the sixpence in 1551. Previously there had been no denomination between the groat and the shilling. It seems likely that the new sixpence replaced devalued testoons (shillings) currently valued at six pennies. The population at this time must have been very confused by the coinage. Edward's new "fine" shillings, sixpences, and three pennies mingled with his father's and his own devalued testoons and groats. At the beginning of Elizabeth's reign the base coins were officially devalued by countermarking. Shillings countermarked with a greyhound's head, for example, were worth $2\frac{1}{2}$d.

The Elizabethan milled sixpences of 1561-71 are very fine coins corresponding to the size of the present shilling. The Queen appears in both a plain and an elaborately decorated dress.

The reverse designs of the sixpence have changed with alarming frequency especially during the present century, although the simple device of the word sixpence within a laurel wreath initiated in 1831 was of long duration, lasting until 1910. The sixpence of George V adopted the royal crest of a lion on crown, becoming a smaller version of the shilling. In 1928 the sixpence was completely redesigned by Kruger Gray and bore a garland of oak leaves and acorns.

The first sixpences of George VI (1937-48) have the imperial cypher GRI beneath a crown. After India left the Empire in 1947, this cypher was no longer appropriate, and the design was replaced by a royal cypher $G^{vi}R$. After 1947 the sixpence like the shilling was no longer a "silver" coin. It was now made of cupro-nickel, an alloy composed of 75% copper and 25% nickel. Previously silver had been seriously debased in 1920. The "silver" coinage of 1922-47 comprised 50% silver and 50% copper.

E. G. Fuller's interesting design for the present Elizabethan sixpence saw the return of a garland — embracing rose, thistle, shamrock and leek.

The Shilling

The word shilling was first used in Anglo-Saxon times as a term to denote money of account, its value originally being five pence, although after the Norman Conquest it became fixed at twelve pence. Henry VII was responsible for striking the first shilling coin in 1504. It was then called a testoon from the Italian *testone* or headpiece. This Milan coin in true Renaissance style attempted a realistic portrait of the monarch to replace the conventional medieval representation. Henry's testoon engraved by Alexander de Brugsal was a finely executed piece with a magnificent profile portrait of the king. This was the first attempt at realistic portraiture in the history of the English coinage.

Henry VIII issued testoons only in 1544. They were large coins with a bearded full face portrait of the king, resembling Holbein's well known painting. Unfortunately they were extremely debased, containing only a third silver — Henry wanted the silver in order to pay for his French wars. It is not surprising that Henry's testoons acquired the nickname 'copper noses', as this feature quickly turned from silver to a coppery hue through wear. John Heywood in an amusing rhyme lampoons them as follows:

Testoons be gone to Oxford, God be their Speede
To study in Brasen nose, there to proceed.
These testoons look redde, how like you the same?
'Tis a token of grace, they blush for shame.

They became extremely unpopular. Even the Church waged war on them. Bishop Latimer preached a fiery sermon on the subject at St. Paul's in 1549 in the presence of the young Edward VI.

The first shillings of Edward VI were struck at the Durham House mint. For the first time in the history of the English coinage a date was featured MD XLVIII. In 1550 the basest silver coins ever to circulate in this country were issued. The silver in these shillings was of 3 oz. fine.

In the following year a serious attempt was made to restore the quality of the coinage to its former fineness. The new fine shilling of Edward VI bore a facing bust of the boy king with a rose on the left and the Roman numeral XII on the right. It is often to be seen in a smooth, worn condition, owing to the fact that it was used in the game of shovelboard or shove groat, the forerunner of our game of shove half penny. Shakespeare knew the coin well. In *Henry IV Part II* we read:

Quoit him down, Bardolph, like a shove-groat shilling.

In the *Merry Wives of Windsor* there is a reference to "two Edward shovelboards" another nickname.

With the exception of the debased currency of Henry VIII and Edward VI the shilling was intrinsically worth twelve pence and only became a token coin at the recoinage which took place in 1816. The first milled shillings were produced by the new screw press and rolling machinery in 1560. Some of the finest shillings ever to circulate were those of Nicholas Briot during the reign of Charles I. Briot was a superb artist and die-cutter who had worked at the Paris mint before being appointed at the Tower. During the Civil War, shillings were struck at a number of provincial mints including York, Shrewsbury, Oxford, Exeter, Bristol, and Lundy Island. Siege pieces valued at a shilling were issued at the besieged towns of Carlisle, Newark, Pontefract, and Scarborough. These were of various shapes and sizes and were hammered out of silver plate. The most common are the lozenge or diamond shaped siege shillings of Newark. They bear a crown on the obverse; the reverse legend reads *OBS : NEWARK 1645.*

Shillings have continued in regular use until the present

16

time. There was one period, however, at the beginning of George III's reign (1760-87) when no silver coins were issued owing to the high price of silver. The sole exception was the so called Northumbrian shilling of 1763, reputed to have been issued as alms to poor Dubliners when the Duke of Northumberland arrived in Ireland in his capacity as Lord Lieutenant.

The well known shilling reverse of a lion over a crown first appeared in 1825 during the reign of George IV and continued in modified form until 1953. The new shilling design by W. Gardner for the coinage of Elizabeth II consisted of a crowned shield bearing three leopards. Since 1937, Scottish shillings have borne a distinctive reverse design. The present Scottish shilling has a shield bearing a lion rampant.

The Florin

The first English florin to be struck was a gold coin of Edward III (1344) and was valued at six shillings. It depicted the king seated beneath a canopy bearing the legend *IHS TRANSIENS PER MEDIUM IBAT* (But Jesus passing through the midst of them went his way).

Almost a hundred years earlier, in 1252, the first gold coins to appear in Europe were struck in Florence. They took the name florin from the city which struck them and became very popular. Undoubtedly the Edward III florin was inspired by the earlier piece.

The silver florin originated in 1849 as a result of public demand for a decimal system to be adopted for the currency. Two parliamentary commissions were set up in 1843 to examine the problem. Sir John Bowring received widespread support in his proposal to introduce a two shilling piece, valued at a tenth of a sovereign, which would eventually replace the half crown, and which would be supplemented later by decimal coins of a smaller denomination. In fact the half crown was not struck between the years 1852 and 1874.

The first issue of the florin, however, aroused public anger and the displeasure of the Queen. The words *DEI GRATIA* (By the Grace of God) and *FIDEI DEFENSOR* (Defender of the Faith) were omitted from the legend. The coins of 1849 are still referred to as "godless" florins. Those of later years retained the Queen's full titles. The new design of the florin embraced floral emblems of the four home countries. A leek appeared for the first time on an English coin.

A double florin was minted in 1887 but was discontinued three years later.

The reverse design of Victoria's Jubilee Coinage florin issued during the years 1887-92 consisted of cruciform shields. This shield design was modified on the florin of the Old Head coinage (1893-1901). The Edward VII florin adopted an entirely new reverse. A tall, striking, windswept figure of Britannia, designed by G. W. de Saulles, appears, modelled from Lady Susan Hicks-Beach, the daughter of the master of the mint.

At the commencement of Queen Elizabeth's reign in 1953, a competition was held amongst artists, who were invited to submit heraldic devices for the reverses of the new coinage. E. G. Fuller was successful in his design for the florin, a double rose in a circlet of thistles, shamrocks and leeks.

A decimal coin of ten new pence has recently come into circulation alongside the florin.

The Half Crown

Gold half crowns were minted during the second coinage of Henry VIII (1526-44). A few years later Edward VI re-introduced the half crown as a silver coin. The first silver half crown was a magnificent piece depicting the king in armour holding a sword, seated on a galloping horse. The shield of the royal arms appeared on the reverse, and has continued to appear on almost all half crowns minted since up to the present day, although the shield takes innumerable forms, especially during Charles I's reign. A notable exception to this rule occurred during the Commonwealth (1649-60). In common with all the denominations except the half penny, the reverse of the Commonwealth half crown bore two adjacent shields of England and Ireland. The overall effect of this design was a pair of breeches. Hence this coinage soon acquired the nickname 'breeches money'.

The shield of the present half crown of Elizabeth II was designed by E. G. Fuller.

The Crown

The first coin to be struck bearing the value of five shillings was the gold half ryal, which appeared in Edward IV's reign. The first actual crown to be minted was a Tudor piece which appeared in 1526. This was also a gold coin and was valued at four shillings and sixpence. It was named Crown of the Rose on account of its design. The obverse bore a crowned shield of the arms of England and the reverse a large rose over a cross. The crown received its name from the French *écu à la couronne,* a contemporary French gold coin displaying a large crown as its chief feature.

Henry VIII's crown was destined only for a short life. In the October of the same year a new crown appeared of increased weight. This was valued at five shillings. The first silver crown was struck by Edward VI in 1551. It was a magnificent coin, showing the king on horseback, the device of the Great Seal of England. It is interesting too in that it is one of the first English coins to bear the date of issue. Similar crowns were issued by James I and Charles I and are highly prized by collectors. Those of Charles were struck not only at the Tower mint, but also on his travels. He had crowns struck at Shrewsbury, Oxford, Truro and Exeter.

Undoubtedly one of the finest crowns produced in the Civil War was Rawlin's pattern crown, struck in 1644. There is a wonderful view of Oxford between the horse's legs including Magdalen Tower and Bridge. Another well known pattern crown, although extremely rare, is the Petition Crown (1663) of Thomas Simon, engraver to the mint. Thomas Simon petitioned the king to compare his trial piece with that of a rival Dutch colleague at the mint, Roettiers. He lost his petition but remained at the mint until he died from the Plague in 1665.

Roettiers' design of four shields set crosswise was permanently adopted for the crown series, and appeared also intermittently on many other coins. It was finally replaced in 1818 by a new design displaying St. George and the Dragon. In mid-Victorian times, however, the crown ceased to be issued on a regular basis on account of its inconvenient size. It has appeared since as a commemoration issue, celebrating such historic occasions as Queen Victoria's jubilee, the accession of George VI, the Festival of Britain (1951), the Coronation of Queen Elizabeth II (1953) and the life of Sir Winston Churchill, the more recent issues being of cupro-nickel.

The Noble and Angel

The noble was a gold coin first issued by Edward III in 1344 valued at half a mark (6/8d.), showing the king standing in a sailing vessel holding a sword and shield. The mark was originally a standard weight of precious metal. In England the mark did not become a coin, but was frequently used as money of account. From the twelfth century onwards it was valued at 13/4d. Legend claims that the design commemorated the great naval battle of Sluys (1340). The entire French fleet was destroyed by Edward's fighting ships commanded by the king in person. Half and quarter nobles were also issued. All had biblical legends. It has been suggested that anyone who contemplated clipping them might have been deterred by realising that they would be guilty of sacrilege.

In 1464 a new gold coinage introduced a new type of noble known as the ryal or rose noble, valued at ten shillings. The design was similar, but the ship has a Yorkist rose amidships, and a flag carrying a large letter E flies at the stern. Half-ryals and quarter-ryals were also minted. The ryal did not replace the old noble, but was supplementary to it, for a new gold coin was issued valued 6/8d. This was the angel, which took its name from the obverse design depicting the Archangel Michael slaying a dragon. The angel became far more popular than the ryal which temporarily disappeared in 1470.

Angels that have been pierced with a hole are frequently encountered. They were used as touch pieces. The king hanged them round the neck of persons suffering from scrofula, a dreaded skin disease very prevalent in the middle ages. This ceremony was known as Touching for the King's Evil. This particular gold coin was supposed to possess a miraculous healing power.

The angel, essentially a medieval coin, assumed a more modern image during the reign of James I. An up-to-date seventeenth century ship appeared in place of a medieval vessel. The coin was eventually discontinued in Charles II's reign, being superseded by the separate issue of gold unites of 20 shillings, crowns and double crowns.

The Sovereign and Guinea

The word pound used in a monetary context originally referred to a pound of silver in weight — that is the amount of silver which could be coined into 240 silver pennies. The word was later adopted to denote a sovereign.

The first gold sovereign was struck by Henry VII in 1489. It had the distinction then of being the largest English coin ever produced and was indeed a magnificent piece. The representation of the sovereign sitting on the throne gave the coin its royal name. The large double Tudor rose on the reverse was equally striking. From 1550 to the end of Queen Elizabeth's reign in 1603 the sovereign was valued at thirty shillings.

James I replaced the sovereign with another gold coin valued at twenty shillings, known as the unite, the unusual name of which was a reference to the recent union with Scotland. A magnificent triple unite showing a half length figure of the king holding a sword was struck at Shrewsbury and also at Oxford during the Civil War by the king.

The modern version of the sovereign, a smaller coin, also

in gold, made its first appearance in 1817. Like the angel it showed a dragon being slain, but this time the deed is being accomplished by St. George rather than St. Michael. Sovereigns continued to be struck for general circulation until 1917, and half sovereigns until 1915. After this date they were struck only for the Bank of England's gold reserves. A million were struck as recently as 1957 for this purpose.

The guinea has a fascinating history. Originally it was introduced in 1663 by Charles II as a gold coin of twenty shillings. The gold for the new coinage was chiefly supplied by the Africa Company which traded in the territory of what is now called Ghana. The land was known as Guinea and later the Gold Coast. The first guineas bore the company's mark, an elephant badge. Although the guinea was legal tender for twenty shillings until 1717, its actual value varied considerably. George I fixed its value at twenty one shillings in that year. For a hundred years the guinea replaced the sovereign as a current coin. It was last minted in 1813.

GREEK AND ROMAN COINS

It is not possible in this booklet to give a full account of the coinages of Classical Greece and Rome. The development of coinage in these two great ancient civilisations will be outlined, albeit briefly.

Greek Coins

The world's first recognisable coins were struck by the Lydians in Asia Minor, in what is now Western Turkey, in the eighth century B.C. The first community in Greece itself to strike coins was the small island of Aegina. They consisted of lumps of silver each stamped on one side with the figure of a turtle, the badge of the island city state. The reverse was left blank. When the turtles, as the coins were known, were first made, they functioned purely as bullion. Later, when it was realised that a profit could be made by valuing them as equivalent to a certain weight of silver (two drachma) and issuing them with less silver content, they became a medium of exchange.

Soon other Greek states began to strike coins, each bearing the city emblem. The Corinthians placed Pegasus, a winged horse, on their coins. They were referred to colloquially as ponies. Corinthian coins were the first to bear a pictorial symbol on the reverse, normally the head of Athene or another goddess. By the beginning of the sixth century B.C., Athens issued its own coinage — the celebrated owls, which were known and accepted throughout Greece.

During the sixth century an increasing number of cities in Central and Southern Greece issued coins, their designs being simple and effective, yet lacking artistry. The Sicilians, however, initiated a coinage more imaginative and artistic and of better execution. The coins of Zancle (Messina) depict the quay, shaped like a sickle, lined with warehouses, enclosing a plunging dolphin. Those of Himera show the local nymph washing in a fountain, as if to invite their possessor to enjoy the city's famous warm springs.

Greek coins reached their zenith in the fifth century B.C., but the series lasts through the Macedonian Empire of Philip and Alexander and the Roman occupation of the Greek world. Its scope is tremendous for, in theory, it embraces not only the coins of Greece and the Peleponnese, but also those of Crete, Asia Minor, Syria, Egypt, Persia, Spain and Gaul. Even coins of the Jews, and of Celtic Britain are included by numismatists in the Greek series.

Greek coins of silver, especially those of fifth century Athens and Sicily, are extremely expensive. One may obtain an interesting selection of bronze coins for a pound or two each. It is not generally realised that Jewish coins in circulation during the life of Christ and shortly afterwards may still be obtained fairly cheaply. The earliest Jewish coins were struck by Simon Maccabaeus (141-135 B.C.), John Hyrcanus (135-104 B.C.) and Alexander Jannaeus (103-76 B.C.). They are small unattractive bronze pieces, very poorly struck. The devices include a poppy head, a palm, an anchor and a wheel. When Judaea became a Roman province after the capture of Jerusalem by Mark Antony in A.D. 37 Roman currency was commonly used, although local bronze coins were struck by Herodias. Local coins were also struck by Roman procurators, including Pontius Pilate. During the years A.D. 66-70, when the Jews were in revolt, a second national coinage was instituted by the Sanhedrin in both silver and bronze. The silver shekel and half shekel depicted a chalice and lily, often referred to as the Rod of Aaron. They bore the date (years 1-5 of the Revolt) and the legend "The Redemption of Zion".

Roman Coins

The Roman series is equally long and varied. Roman coins were struck from early Republican times (269 B.C.) until the late Empire (476 A.D.) a period of almost 750 years. The earlier Republican silver coins depicted the two headed Janus and Jupiter in a quadriga (a chariot drawn by four horses).

At the end of the third century B.C. the first silver denarius was struck. This was a 10 as piece. The weight of the as was fixed at an ounce. The denarius was the forerunner of the medieval European denier and the English penny. The first denarii showed the helmeted head of Roma on the obverse and Castor and Pollux riding into battle on the reverse. As Rome's power increased, branch mints were established to supplement the output of the central mint at Rome. It became customary for mint masters to put their own names on the coins. New designs appeared, the finest being Diana, the goddess of the chase, driving a two horse chariot and Hercules driving two centaurs, half man, half horse. By the end of the second century B.C., the mint masters, proud of their glorious heritage, struck coins depicting scenes from their family history.

Some of the commoner types of Roman Republican coins may be obtained for a few pounds from reputable dealers.

Coins of the Empire are even commoner. They regularly occur in "finds" in Great Britain each year. Often hoards consist of several hundreds, even thousands, of coins. Coins of the Empire flooded into this country in very large numbers for almost four hundred years.

Those of the early Empire are of tremendous historical interest. In an age lacking television, radio, newspapers and magazines, coins constituted the sole mass medium of advertising. Emperors treated their coinage with the respect that governments treat television today. A striking portrait on the obverse linked with an important message on the reverse was considered as essential an ingredient of the public image as a good television image is now. Frequent changes of coin type ensured the maintenance of public interest at peak level.

Roman governments awed their subjects throughout the Empire by providing them with a variety of beautifully sculptured heads on their coins. They were kept well informed of current events by a startling array of fascinating reverses — anniversaries and commemorations, victories in battle, propagandist exhortations to uphold the traditional Roman virtues, important social reforms, even building programmes. Undoubtedly coins were the chief vehicle of Roman political propaganda.

Collectors have an endless choice of exciting themes within this series. They may choose to collect coins of a particular Emperor or period. If finances permit, they may try to form a portrait gallery of the early emperors including Julius Caesar, Augustus, Claudius, Nero, Trajan and Hadrian. A bronze and silver piece of most emperors may still be obtained for a few pounds.

During the first and second centuries A.D. most of the coinage was produced at the mints in Rome. Originally the bronze was minted in a separate mint controlled by the Senate. Thus bronze coins of the period bear the letters S.C. (by order of the Senate). During the third and fourth centuries a process of decentralisation occurred and more than twenty imperial mints operated in towns as far apart as London and Antioch, Arles and Alexandria.

A brief summary of the relationship between the denominations from Augustus may be helpful.

4 quadrants or 2 semisses = 1 as
4 assess or 2 dupondii = 1 sestertius
4 sestertii = 1 denarius
25 denarii = 1 aureus.

The as and its fractional coins were of copper, the dupondius and sestertius of orichalchum (a golden brass), the denarius of silver, and the aureus of gold.

Many collectors attempt to obtain a silver and a brass or copper coin of each of the twelve Caesars, a remarkable portrait gallery indeed. Several pounds, however, may be necessary to purchase one or two of the series. The silver denarius of Tiberius has become expensive on account of its tremendous Christian significance. It is probably the piece used as tribute money and referred to in the well-known account of Christ's approach to the problem of our responsibility to the State and to God. The story is told in three of the four gospels — Matthew XXII 19, Mark XII 15, and Luke XX 24. The coin asked for by Christ bore the Emperor's portrait, as the Gospel accounts inform us, and the reverse depicts his mother Livia. The obverse legend reads *TI CAESAR DIVI AUG F AUGUSTUS* (Tiberius Caesar Augustus Son of the Divine Augustus) — Tiberius' "superscription"!

The reverse types of the imperial coins are of great variety and interest. A collection of these can be built up at a very reasonable cost. Roman coins were minted in such vast quantities that commoner types of antoniniani of the third and fourth centuries embracing many reverse types may be obtained for a few shillings each. Antoniniani were originally of silver, but from the time of Gallienus (260-268 A.D.) they became small bronze coins. They are now referred to as "third brass".

An equally interesting representative collection of mints could be built up of coins of this period, or perhaps a selection of coins of a particular mint such as London. You may wish to study the coinage of a specific emperor. Antoniniani of Gallienus (260-268), Tetrius I (270-273), Probus (276-282) and Constantine the Great (306-337) are particularly plentiful.

HOARDS

Numismatics or the study of coins is making an increasing contribution to history and archaeology. A headline in the daily paper that I picked up this morning reads "Canute coin find points to Saxon settlement. . . . The discovery of a coin of King Canute indicates that a Saxon settlement existed on a site thought previously only to have been a medieval extension of the town". Undoubtedly coins are invaluable dating evidence, and archaeologists are profoundly happy when a coin or group of coins is discovered, especially when it is sealed. Casual finds may be extremely misleading.

If one is fortunate to find an ancient or medieval coin in the ground or even on the surface, one should always make a note of the exact location spot and the circumstances in which it was found, before reporting the find to the local museum.

It is even more important to record and report finds of coin hoards. Several extremely exciting hoards have been revealed during the past few years including the largest find of medieval gold coins ever recorded in England (Fishpool, Notts. 1966).

There has been a certain amount of misunderstanding concerning the reporting of hoards, so it might be advisable to state the position. It is a serious offence not to declare a coin find. If the coroner declares the find to be Treasure Trove, generous compensation is given to the finder, not the owner of the ground. Treasure Trove may be defined as a hoard of gold or silver (bullion, objects or coins) which has been deliberately deposited in the ground, the owner of which cannot be traced. It is worth noting that copper and bronze coinage are outside the terms of reference. The coroner must be quite sure that the coins or objects found were not casually lost or thrown away.

When a hoard has been claimed by the Crown, it is normal practice for the British Museum to retain a selection of coins required for the national collection; other interesting coins will be allotted to local collections and the remainder returned to the finder. Before the coins are dispersed, however, a full analysis of the hoard is made. This is known as hoard evidence. In the last century many important hoards were incompletely recorded, and this vital evidence is now lost for ever.

There are three chief causes of hoarding coinage: safety in time of war, safety in a period of economic crisis, and saving in time of peace. Most hoards were probably motivated by a combination of the first two causes. J. D. A. Thompson has written "The reigns of the three Edwards are, with the exception of the Civil Wars of Charles I, the most prolific in coin finds since the Romano-British period — due to a period of continual unrest and bad economic conditions".

A study of hoards has proved of help to the scholar in innumerable ways. Students of Anglo Saxon and medieval coinage have been enabled, by studying hoard evidence, to arrange the issues in chronological order. It is often difficult to date a hoard with absolute precision. Numismatists usually have to decide which is the latest coin in the hoard, and accept that the hoard was probably buried shortly after its minting. As new issues occurred every two or three years, and coins of previous issues were recalled at the same time, the composition of Saxon and Norman hoards is fairly regular. In order to establish chronology numismatists look for muling of types and for die-links. Muling is the term used when an obverse of one coin is linked with a reverse type normally associated with a previous monarch. The discovery of mules helps to establish two succeeding issues. The term die-link refers to two coins which have been struck from identical dies. These are revealed by identical flaws in the design.

The following brief notes on a few outstanding hoards may be of interest:

Carrawburgh 1897 near Hadrian's Wall

This vast hoard of 16,000 Roman coins spanning almost two hundred years (A.D. 100-300) was found on the site of a well dedicated to a British water nymph Corentina. These coins were thrown into the well as good luck offerings to the goddess.

Cuerdale 1840 near Preston, Lancs.

99% of all known Viking coins struck in Britain are from this hoard of 7,000 coins and 1,000 oz. of silver ingots discovered on the lands of Cuerdale Hall farm on the banks of the Ribble. This hoard is virtually the sole source of information concerning the Viking coinage of the late ninth century. The coins had been originally enclosed in a lead lined box, probably a military pay chest. It has been estimated that the hoard was buried during the reign of Edward the Elder (900-925) as his are the latest coins in the hoard. An analysis of the hoard by Lyon and Stewart reveals that it contained pennies of the Archbishop of Canterbury (67), Wessex (66), Mercia (2), East Anglia (27), the Vikings (4,856), continental coins (1,024), and oriental coins (27). Many mysteries are still to be unravelled, but one of the chief lessons of this hoard is the widespread distribution of coinage during this period.

Beaworth 1833 Hampshire

Between 8,000 and 12,000 English silver pennies and cut half pennies of William I and his son Rufus were involved in the Beaworth hoard which must have been deposited about 1087. Of these 6,282 have been recorded. As in the Cuerdale find, a lead chest originally contained the coins. The coins were accidentally discovered by some boys one Sunday afternoon, playing near the village pond. Many were skimmed over the pond as missiles, before their interest and value were realised. The vast majority of Beaworth coins belong to the last type of William the Conqueror known as the Pax penny. Almost all known Pax pennies in museums and private collections come from this hoard.

Tealby 1807 Lincolnshire

The Tealby hoard gives its name to the Tealby coinage of Henry II — that is the first issue (1154-80). Tealby coins are uncommon. They would be more plentiful if 5,127 had not been melted at the Tower!

Tutbury 1831 Staffordshire

Edward I and II pennies are still quite common. This state of affairs owes much to the Tutbury find, for 20,000 coins were buried in this hoard, most of which were Edward pennies and only a small proportion found their way to the British Museum. It is interesting to note firstly that almost all the mints in operation during this period are represented in the hoard and secondly that Scottish, Irish and over a thousand foreign coins were included as well.

Fishpool 1966 Nottinghamshire

1,237 medieval gold coins were unearthed on a building site at Fishpool near Newstead Abbey on March 22nd, 1966. No less than six persons were involved in the find of whom only two received full market value, because of their promptness in reporting the hoard. Several hitherto "unknown" coins appeared at Fishpool, including a quarter-noble of Edward IV.

JETTONS

There are numerous types of pieces, closely resembling coins, but which cannot, strictly speaking, be classed as currency. These include theatre passes, hop tokens, communion tokens, advertisement counters and jettons. They all have their devotees, but in the main they are ignored by collectors and students.

It is rather strange that jettons and counters have failed to attract serious attention in this country, for they are of immense interest, and offer an exciting field for research. The collector who is frustrated in his attempt to build up a comprehensive collection of medieval coins by his limited resources might well think of turning to counters. A good collection of medieval counters can still be formed at a very low cost.

Jettons are of interest to the historian and the mathematician as well as to the numismatist, for they throw some light on a number of important aspects of economic life in medieval Europe including the techniques used in medieval accountancy and the development of the English exchequer in the thirteenth and fourteenth centuries.

In the middle ages all arithmetical calculations had to be worked out in Roman figures, as our present Hindu-Arabic numerals were not in common use in northern Europe before the seventeenth century. Thus the counting board or chequer board was an essential item of equipment in every medieval tavern, shop and business house, taking the form of a rectangular table ruled with lines or squares. The illustration shows a sixteenth century counter made by Hans Krauwinckel of Nuremberg. A German business man is seen working out his accounts on the counter board. He is casting his counters on to the chequered or squared cloth and will record the totals, in Roman figures of course, in the open notebook on his left. His money bag is close to his right elbow!

Jettons were thrown on to the lines or spaces, as shown in the figures below. When adding, the medieval accountant would start on the bottom line by shifting the counters in both the first two columns into the third. He knew that no more than four counters should be placed on a line, and no more than one in a space. Thus the accountant need only be able to count up to five.

28

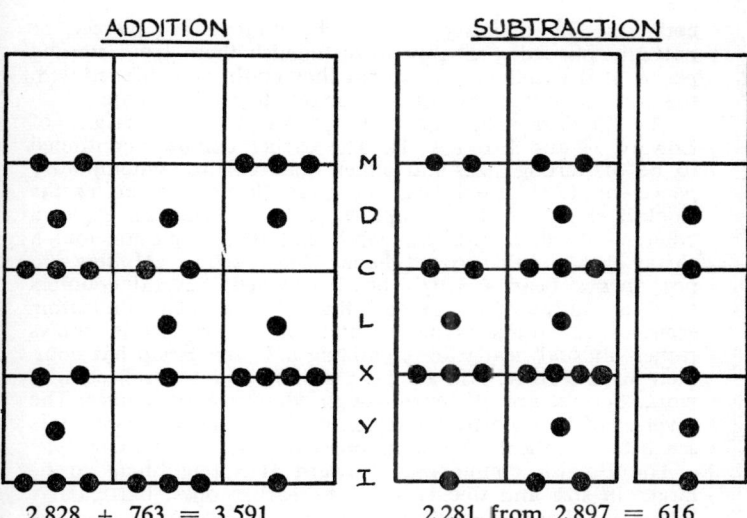

ADDITION				SUBTRACTION			

2,828 + 763 = 3,591   2,281 from 2,897 = 616

The use of the chequer board

In subtracting, the lower number was set out in the first column. A simple process of cancelling took place, again commencing at the bottom line, and after the corresponding jettons in both columns had been removed, the answer remained in the second column.

Even the royal accounts were cast on a huge chequer board at Westminster by the Chancellor of the "Exchequer". Accounts were submitted twice a year by the sheriffs at the exchequer board. It is thought that the system of exchequer reckoning and audit was introduced into England by a minister of Henry I, Bishop Roger of Salisbury who had learnt it in his home town of Caen.

English Counters

It is known that actual coins were first used on English chequer boards including the Royal Exchequer Board at Westminster — the sterling pennies of the reigning monarch. The first true English counters appeared during the reign of Edward I (1280). They were struck in brass and were modelled on the contemporary sterling pence. Lawrence has shown that identical punches were used for both coins and counters. The majority of English counters are pierced or partially pierced, probably to distinguish them from sterling pence. It is extremely likely that they could be confused with the current coinage by peasants unable to read or write.

The English series continued throughout the reigns of Edward II and Edward III. The earlier counters continued to be of sterling size, and either imitated the contemporary pence or bore interesting medieval devices including the English shield or three leopards, a lion's head, an eagle, a counter board, a rose, the lamb and flag, a gorgoneion, a castle or a broad arrow (pheon). The portrait counters did not always bear a king's head crowned. Several counters bear a mitred head rather than a crowned, indicating ecclesiastical usage. One counter in my collection shows rather unusual headgear resembling a Robin Hood hat complete with feather. Not all these sterling counters reflect mint work. Several are obviously rough contemporary copies. The reverses of both portrait and non portrait Edwardian counters are often identical. The commonest reverse is a cross moline.

The English counters of Edward III's reign tend to be larger in size and thicker than the earlier ones. Particularly interesting are the wardrobe counters issued for use on the chequer board of the King's wardrobe, an office responsible for the personal finances of the royal household. Other late English coins, more commonly encountered, depict the king standing and seated beneath a canopy. These bear a legend *GRA REX*. They closely resemble unpierced French counters which normally read *DE LA TONE* (made of latten).

The English series seems to end at the close of the fourteenth century, being replaced by the more abundant French, Tournai, and Nuremburg jettons. English counters, unfortunately, are not very common, but you may be lucky enough to come across one or two.

French and Flemish Jettons

Much more common are French jettons. About the year 1400 France seems to have gained a monopoly in the manufacture of counters. They were used in every European country including England during the fifteenth and sixteenth centuries. They are of immense interest and variety. Early ones of the Chambre de Monnaies (the Treasury) show a crude pair of scales. Later ones show bear baiting, crowns, dolphins (counters of the Dauphine), the lamb and flag, monogram of Jesus, monogram of Maria, the letter V (representing the Virgin Mary) and shields and badges of every description. Religious devices predominate. I possess a particularly interesting jetton showing a squirrel eating a nut, and the legend *AVE MARIA PLENA GRACIA* (Hail Mary, full of grace). Sometimes French jettons warned their owners not to use them as coins. Several proclaim that they are made only of base metal *DE LATONI* (of latten). The legend of another *VIVE BLAN* [ ] *PAIN* (long live white bread!) is not an advertisement slogan to increase the sale of bread, but a pun on the issuer's name. Jean Blancpain was a die-cutter at the Paris mint who manufactured jettons for private sale without authority. His house was raided in 1434, and dies and punches were seized by government officials. The legend on the counter may well have given him away.

Large numbers of Flemish counters also appeared during the fourteenth and fifteenth centuries. Many were struck at Tournai, the centre of the copper mining industry. They frequently imitate French jettons in design, but tend to be thicker and cruder.

You will be able to obtain an interesting selection of French and Flemish counters for a few pence or a few shillings each, according to condition, from coin dealers. It is rewarding sometimes to sieve through the junk boxes or saucers in antique shops and discover medieval counters among the masses of Victorian farthings and three penny bits.

Nuremburg Jettons

A few citizens of Nuremburg, an important trading centre, gradually gained complete control of counter manufacturing during the sixteenth century. They were not afraid to advertise their names on the counters, the principal issuers being Hans and Egidius Krauwinckel, Hans and Georges Schultes, Kilianus Koch, Valentius Maler and Wolf Laufer.

Nuremburg counters are extremely common, and have been found in large numbers in this country, specially on the sites of abbeys. They can be easily recognised by the following features. Although they have the appearance of coins, they bear no value, they are normally of brass of varying diameter, crude and extremely thin. The legend usually includes the issuer's name and his native town of Nuremburg spelt in a variety of ways. The commonest type of stock jetton carried the design of three open crowns and three fleurs de lys arranged in the form of a circle round a rose. The city emblem, a crowned orb known as Reichsapfel, appears on the reverse. The legends are varied and usually have a religious message such as *GOTES SEGEN MACHT REICH* (God's blessing maketh rich). Or the more serious *HEIT RODT MORGEN TODT* (Today red, tomorrow dead).

Vast quantities of jettons of larger types also exist. The two which you are most likely to come across are those showing a sailing vessel at sea, and those depicting the winged lion of Venice. One particularly common type of ship counter was manufactured for the French market. Its legend reads *VOLEVE LA GALLEE DE FRANCE* (Let the French galley sail). A diamond or lozenge of the coat of arms of France (shown as four fleurs de lys) appears on the reverse. Most ship counters are signed by Hans Schultes, although some were made by Damianus and Hans Krauwinckel.

Undoubtedly Hans Krauwinckel was the finest craftsman of the Nuremburg makers. His counters depicting the winged lion of Venice holding a bible are of a far higher standard of execution than cruder copies made by Hans and Georges Schultes. Krauwinckel made several series of handsome jettons especially with collectors in mind, embracing the Old Testament, Classical Mythology, Roman History, and the contemporary political scene. These jettons are well worth collecting and may sometimes be picked up quite cheaply. They can often be identified by the maker's initials H.K. in the exergue (the bottom section of the coin). Some of them bear dates, the most frequent being 1589 and 1601. The counters of the classical series show well known scenes and figures from classical mythology including Romulus and Remus, Apollo and Diana, Pluto, Jupiter, Minerva, and Vulcan. The biblical series is especially interesting and comprehensive embracing Adam and Eve, Daniel in the Lions' Den and the Crucifixion.

TOKENS

Traders' tokens have been issued at various times in our history. Some are even current today. There are three periods in particular when the issuing of tokens by tradesmen was practised on a large scale — the middle of the seventeenth century (1648-72), the end of the eighteenth century (1787-97) and the beginning of the nineteenth century (1811-16). The fascinating tokens produced during these periods were by no means just collectors' pieces or even advertisement counters. They were current coins and essential to local economy during periods of political, social and economic unrest.

A mint workshop in the sixteenth century (from an old French print).
The mintmaster is giving instructions to one of his workmen.
The moneyer on the left is trimming the blanks, the one in the centre
preparing them, and the one on the right is about to strike a coin.

An eighteenth century screwpress (from the Universal Magazine).

A milled sixpence of Queen Elizabeth I (1562). The mint mark is a star. The Tudor rose is unusually large.

A Viking silver penny of Cnut, struck at York about 891.

A silver penny of William I struck by Swegn at Bristol, known as a Paxs penny as these letters appear on the reverse.

A silver denarius of Vespasian (69-79 A.D.). The legend reads (from right to left) IMP. CAESAR VESPASIANUS AUG. Vespasian as a young man commanded a section of the invasion force of Britain under Claudius. As his portrait shows, he was sixty years of age, when he was proclaimed emperor.

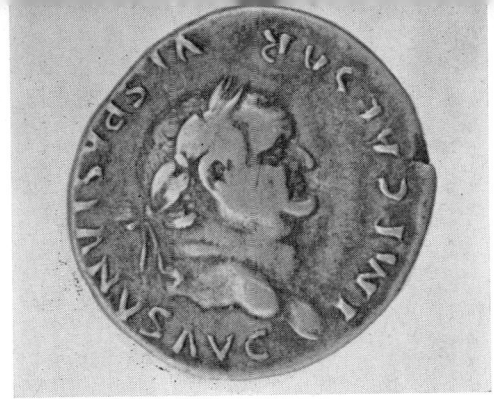

An as of Claudius (41-54 A.D.). The legend reads TI CLAUDIUS CAESAR AUG P. M. TR. P. IMP. Caesar was the personal name or cognomen of the Julia family. Claudius was entitled to use this name as a member of the Julia family. Augustus was a title of honour. P.M. stands for Pontifex Maximum, another imperial title. TR. P. refers to the power of the Tribune, an imperial office. Claudius was responsible for the successful invasion of Britain in A.D. 43.

A dupondius of Nero (54-68 A.D.). It bears the legend NERO CLAUDIUS CAESAR AUG GERMANI. Nero was adopted by Claudius in A.D. 50. He had a chequered career of cruelty and tyranny. He murdered his own mother and his first wife and eventually committed suicide.

A base shilling of Edward VI (1550-53).
A 'Fine' shilling of Edward VI (1551-53).

A Newark siege piece of 1645 valued at a shilling, hammered out of silver plate. This is the reverse side.

A shilling of Charles I struck at the Tower mint.

Seventeenth century inn tokens of High Wycombe, Bucks

Obverse of token of Richard Lucas of the Red Lion:
RATHER DEAD THAN DISLOYAL.

Obverse of token of Thomas Butterfield of the Wheatsheaf:
THO. BUTTERFIELD.

Obverse of token of Jeremiah Gray of the Swan:
JEREMIAH GRAY IN.

A Nuremburg "Rechenmeister" jetton of 1553, showing a businessman working at his accounts on the exchequer board. His notebook is open for him to record the totals in Roman figures. His moneybag is also at hand!

A Nuremburg jetton of Hans Krauwinckel, showing the winged lion of Venice. The obverse legend refers to the Apostle, St. Mark. The arms of Nuremburg, a crowned orb, appear on the reverse.

A fourteenth century French jetton, depicting an open crown, and bearing the religious legend AVE MARIA (Hail Mary).

An English counter of Edward I, struck from the same punches as those used on the dies of the contemporary sterling pence minted at London. Notice the central piercing, typical of this series; also the absence of legend.

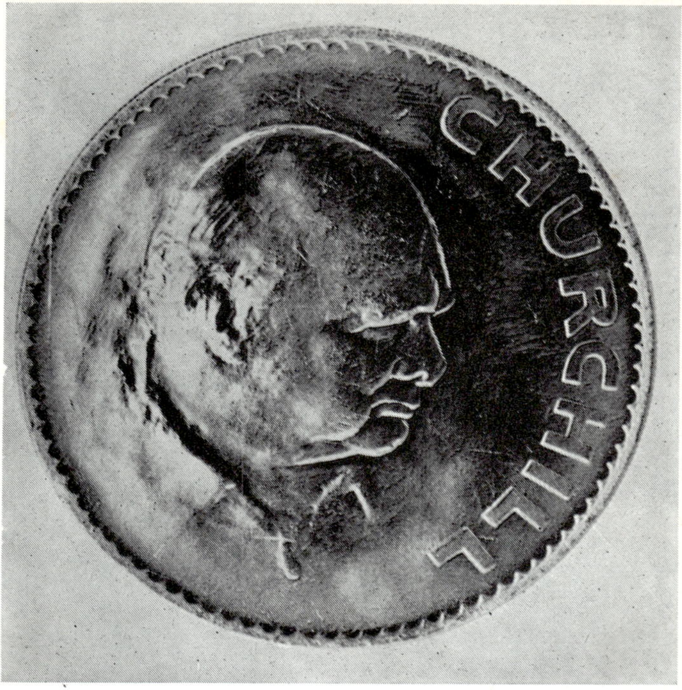

The commemorative crown of Sir Winston Churchill. You are looking at the reverse of the coin, for according to numismatic convention the obverse shows the sovereign's head.

Ten New Pence piece (1968) (replacing the florin). The obverse shows the standard Commonwealth effigy of the queen by Mr. Arnold Machin. The reverse design of a crowned lion (part of the English crest) is by Mr. Christopher Ironside.

Seventeenth century tokens

The tokens of the seventeenth century appeared just after the Civil War because of the persistent refusal of the government to issue an official copper currency to function as small change. It has been estimated that about 12,000 types of tokens were issued during the years 1648-72 by shop-keepers, tavern keepers and traders of every description in villages, towns and cities throughout the country. Most of them were valued at a farthing or a half penny. They were chiefly made of copper or brass—hence the term 'brass farthing'.

The tokens of this period may be recognised by the following features. They usually carry the name of the issuer, his town, the arms or symbol of his trade, the initials of the issuer and his wife and the value of the token.

One token of Bishops Stortford in Hertfordshire reads:

Obv. *SIMON RUTLAND IN The Grocers Arms*
Rev. *BISHOPS STORTFORD*   *S.T.R.*

We can deduce from this that the issuer was Simon Rutland, a Bishops Stortford grocer, and that his wife's christian name began with T. The parish registers confirm that his wife's name was Thomasin.

London tokens, of which there were several thousand, normally bear the name of the street rather than the town. Tavern tokens often carry only the initials of the issuer as for example:

Obv. *AT THE COK AND BULL*
Rev. *NEER THE IRON GATE*   *H.I.M.*

One is then challenged to try and discover the identity of H.M. and his wife!

Seventeenth century tokens had a limited circulation. An extract from Evelyn's Diary seems to confirm the fact that they were essentially a local coin. "Payable through the neighbourhood, though seldom reaching farther than the next street or two".

Traders and tavern keepers kept sorting trays on their counters so that when a sufficient number of tokens had been received, they could be redeemed at the place of issue.

These tokens are of particular interest to the local historian. They help him to gain a picture of local trade in shops and taverns. In a study of the tokens of High Wycombe in Buckinghamshire, for example, I was enabled to discover a great deal about the background of the issuers by undergoing research into parish registers, ledger books, wills, hearth tax records and quarter session records.

I discovered that most of the traders who issued the tokens were prominent business men of their day and well known in High Wycombe. Thirteen of the twenty two were elected burgers, eight became aldermen, and four mayor. Richard Lucas of the Red Lion in the High Street became Mayor three times. On one occasion (15th December, 1672) he was one of two rival Mayors who were simultaneously elected to office!

Of the seven innkeepers who issued tokens it was possible to locate the site of all their inns, despite the fact that only one still functioned as an inn. The Antelope of Robert Whitton, for instance, now forms part of a jeweller's shop in the High Street. It was originally the forerunner of the Royal Military Academy at Sandhurst.

Seventeenth century tokens in Very Fine condition may still be obtained for thirty shillings, and will pose problems that will keep you absorbed for years. You will probably wish to limit your collection to the tokens of your town or county.

Eighteenth and Nineteenth century tokens

The tokens of the eighteenth and nineteenth centuries paint a fascinating picture of the era of the Industrial Revolution. They depict the factories, textile machinery, canals and stage coaches. Those issued in the industrial towns of the Midlands and the North were freely circulated as coins as their wear demonstrates. Particularly interesting and prolific are the Anglesey Parys mine tokens coined in Birmingham and the tokens of John Wilkinson the ironmaster. Wilkinson lacked modesty. His "regal" portrait adorns the obverse of all his tokens. The legend reads *JOHN WILKINSON IRONMASTER*. A particularly graphic reverse depicts a tilt hammer in operation at one of his forges. No scenes of smelting, however, appear on the tokens of the Anglesey Copper Mining Company. Thomas Williams simply put a druid on his tokens, together with a monogram. It has been estimated that over 300 tons of these Anglesey tokens were issued.

The tokens struck by Skidmore and others in London were often struck specifically for collectors, and were not really intended to go into circulation as currency. They are of great interest on account of their views of contemporary buildings in London and other towns.

Commoner varieties of eighteenth and nineteenth century tokens may still be obtained from dealers for a few shillings each.

FORMING A COLLECTION

There are many compelling reasons for forming a collection. I hope that investment will not be a primary one, although it may well be a secondary one! Many collectors place too great a stress on the future value of their pieces. When they purchase a coin they are primarily concerned with its current and prospective market value, rather than the historical perspective which it provides. If one is to progress as a numismatist one must have the right priorities!

If you are to find your collecting intellectually stimulating and of lasting value, I strongly advise you to select a series or topic that will provide you with opportunities for discovery and research. Professional numismatists need not have a monopoly in this matter. Amateur numismatists in recent years, as well as in the past, have become recognised experts in their own specialist sphere, and have written authoritative works on a diversity of subjects.

Most people start collecting very haphazardly. Their collection is of a very general nature and may embrace Roman bronze pieces, Edward pence, Nuremburg jettons, seventeenth and eighteenth century tokens, "cartwheel" pennies of 1797, and modern commemorative crowns. The formation of a general collection can be an invaluable exercise, for it enables the collector to see where his real interests lie, and what he can afford to collect. It may be several years before some form of specialisation is adopted, but this is an essential step if the collector is to graduate to a student. Many specialist collectors of long years standing still retain their original general collection and add to it from time to time, but their greatest delight is in studying their particular field of interest.

It may be argued that today's high prices make it impossible for a beginner, particularly if he is a youngster without capital, to form a worthwhile and interesting collection of any series. Certainly one could not expect him to select such series as Celtic, Roman Republican, Anglo Saxon, or the coinage of Charles I. Even such fascinating series as shortcross and longcross are becoming out of bounds. What remains?

Here are a few suggestions of some inexpensive areas, where the thrill of the chase may be combined with fruitful research. It must be admitted however, that if you rate high artistic merit as a prime consideration in your collecting these suggestions should be ignored.

1) Roman forgeries of 1st century A.D., particularly of the *as* and *dupondius* of Claudius. A fascinating study of degradation.

2) 3rd century bronze *antoniniani* of the Roman emperors.

You may wish to make a study of a particular emperor, or the immense richness of reverse designs, demanding a deep insight into Roman mythology or military history. You might well collect coins of a particular mint such as London or Triers.

3) *Barbarous radiates* of the third and fourth centuries A.D.

Much remains to be discovered concerning these British copies.

4) Silver pennies of Edward I.

This is probably the only medieval silver coinage which can be collected at reasonable cost. The discovery of vast hoards of these pennies, as at Tutbury, accounts for their frequency.

5) Medieval jettons.

This is a much neglected side of numismatics. Large numbers can still be obtained cheaply. Further research is needed into their use, their designs, their manufacture, places of minting. A comprehensive catalogue of the English series is urgently needed.

6) Seventeenth century trade tokens.

This series will provide endless hours of enjoyment to those interested in local history. They will probably wish to collect the tokens of their own town or county, and to find out as much as possible concerning the background of the issuers. Original research can be undertaken, using parish registers, wills and inventories, hearth tax records, quarter session records. For those more interested in technical numismatic matters, few counties have had their tokens faithfully catalogued in detail. Close study of border patterns will provide clues as to dating the undated tokens, and a study of die-links will help to solve many problems concerning their manufacture and distribution.

7) Victorian advertisement "Counters", Hop Tokens and Inn Tallies.

Like the tokens above, these often prove of great assistance to the student of local history.

This is by no means an exhaustive list of suggestions. On holiday recently I came across bread tokens, issued by the Church of San Salvador in Bruges. I bought several very cheaply from an antique shop near the church, and immediately a new interest and line of enquiry was opened up.

A few notes concerning the housing of the collection might be helpful. Undoubtedly the most satisfactory method is a wooden cabinet, which may be obtained from a dealer or auctioneer. Cabinets of oak should be avoided at all costs, as deterioration of the coins will result. Unfortunately cabinets are quite expensive. You may prefer to spend your money on coins rather than on the cabinet! The best alternative is the coin album, which can be readily obtained from dealers. One great advantage which an album possesses is that both sides of the coin may be easily studied. Another is that the coins need not be handled by over enthusiastic friends.

Whether you choose an album or a cabinet, careful records must be kept. Brief details of the coin including monarch, date, issue and denomination should be available close to the coin itself. In a separate card index file, the results of your researches should be recorded. Methodical filing will save hours of frustration later.

Make certain that your coins are fully insured, both in the house and when transported. A separate insurance policy is normally required for valuable items such as coins. Do not assume that your normal household policy will cover your coin collection.

You are strongly advised not to clean your coins unless it is absolutely necessary. Never polish them. Dirt should be removed from coins of all metal by washing them in soapy water, and brushing them with an old tooth brush. Corrosion in copper coins may be tackled gently with a bone needle.

Very little has been said about where coins for your collection may be obtained. You may be fortunate in having been given or bequeathed a nucleus of interesting coins on which to build your collection. There are still boxes of coins lying idle and unnoticed in many attics and outhouses. If you choose to collect Victorian advertisement counters, you may find local antique shops, market stalls or even junk shops prove fruitful. The collector of Roman coins, Edward pennies and seventeenth century tokens on the other hand will have to rely on reputable dealers for most of his acquisitions. There are several of longstanding in London, and a number in the provinces. If you are in doubt, it would be wise to seek advice from the secretary of your local numismatic society. It would be a good idea in any case to join a local society, the details of which can usually be obtained from your local library. You will then be able to meet fellow enthusiasts, listen to talks and join in discussions.

FURTHER READING

BOOKS

GENERAL

Milne, Sutherland and Thompson *Coin Collecting* 1950

Chamberlain, C. C. *The Teach Yourself Guide to Numismatics* 1960

Carson, R. A. G. *Coins — Ancient, Medieval and Modern* 1962

Whitting, P. D. *Coins in the Classroom* 1966

Jacobs, K. A. *Coins and Christianity* 1959

ENGLISH

Seaby, P. *The Story of English Coinage* 1952

Oman, C. *The Coinage of England* 1931

Brooke, G. C. *English Coins* 3rd Ed. 1950

Mack, R. P. *The Coinage of Ancient Britain* 1953

North, J. J. *English Hammered Coins* 1960

Peck, C. W. *English Copper, Tin and Bronze Coins in the British Museum 1558-1958* 2nd Ed. 1966

Josset, C. R. *Money in Britain* 1962

GREEK & ROMAN

Seltman, C. *Greek Coins* 1955

Mattingley, H. *Roman Coins* 1960

Klawans, Z. H. *Reading and Dating Imperial Coins* 1953

Askew, G. *The Coinage of Roman Britain* 1951

Grant, M. *Roman History from Coins* 1958

JETTONS & TOKENS

Barnard, F. P. *The Casting Counter and The Counting Board* 1916 (out of print)

Boyne, W. *Trade Tokens issued in the Seventeenth Century* (ed. G. C. Williamson) 1889. Recently reprinted in 3 vols.

Mathias, P. *English Trade Tokens* 1962

Rowe, C. M. *Salisbury's Local Coinage* 1966

PERIODICALS

Monthly bulletins issued by dealers: —

Messrs. Spinks' *Numismatic Circular*

Messrs. Seaby's *Coin and Medal Bulletin*

Weekly Newspaper: *Coins Medals and Currency*

Monthly Magazines: *Coins and Medals, Coin Monthly*

Annual Publications:

Cunobelin (British Association of Numismatic Societies)

Numismatic Chronicle (Royal Numismatic Society)

British Numismatic Journal (British Numismatic Society)

GAZETTEER

Doubtful mints are not included. This is by no means an exhaustive list of important hoards and museums. Lack of space demands the selection of but a few of the more significant. Most museums have general collections. Reference is made here to features of particular interest. Normally only a small selection of coins is on display in museums. If you wish to study others, it is advisable to write to the curator, requesting permission to look at them at his convenience. It will help him considerably if you state the particular coins or series of coins in which you are interested.

Abbreviations and terms:

S—Saxon.

N—Norman.

Dep.—deposited. The year given is an approximate one.

Edward C. — Edward the Confessor.

The number in brackets indicates the number of moneyers operating during the coinage of Aethelred II — Edward the Confessor or Harold II or during specified Norman coinages. This will help to give a comparison of the importance of individual Saxon and Norman mints.

Tealby — The first coinage of Henry II.

Shortcross — Coinage of 1180-1247 (Richard I to Henry III), so called because of the short cross on the reverse.

Longcross — Coinage of 1247-1272 (Henry III to Edward I), so called because of the long cross on the reverse.

I am indebted to J. D. A. Thompson's *Inventory of Coin Hoards* for much of the information concerning hoards.

Bedfordshire

Mint	Bedford **S** Edwig – Harold II (21), **N** William I – II (4), Henry I (1), Stephen (1).
Hoard	Ampthill (1836) 146 Tealby (dep. 1168 – 79).
	Steppingley (1912) 518 Shortcross and Longcross.
Society	Bedford N.S.

Berkshire

Mints	Reading **S** Edward C. Only 1 coin known. Mediaeval Coins of Abbot of Reading. (Edward III.)
	Wallingford **S** Aethelstan –Harold II (28), **N** William I and II (9), Henry I (5), Tealby (1), Longcross (4).

Hoard	Newbury (1756) 3499 pence of Edward I and II.
Museum	Reading Museum — Miscellaneous.
Society	Reading Coin Club.

Buckinghamshire

Mints	Aylesbury **S** Aethelred II – Edward C (8).
	Buckingham **S** Edward the Martyr – Edward C (6).
Museum	County Museum, Aylesbury — Miscellaneous.
Societies	Bucks N.S.; Beaconsfield N.S.

Cambridgeshire

Mint	Cambridge **S** Edgar – Harold II (29), **N** William I – II **(5).**
Museum	Fitzwilliam Museum, Cambridge — Large collections of all periods.
Society	Cambridgeshire N.S. (Cambridge).

Cheshire

Mint	Chester **S** Aethelstan – Harold II (42), **N** William I – II (14), Henry I (10), Stephen (4), Tealby (2), Edward I.
	Civil War Chester (1644).
	Recoinage of William III (1695).
Hoards	Chester No. 3. (Aug. 1914) 122 Saxon pence Edgar – Aethelred II.
	Chester No. 4. (Nov. 1952) 525 Saxon pence. Dep. 970.
Museum	Grosvenor Museum, Chester. – Roman, Willoughby – Gardner collection of Chester Mint.
Society	Lancs. and Cheshire N.S. (Manchester).

Cornwall

| Mint | Launceston **S** Aethelred II (1), **N** William I – II (2), Stephen (1), Tealby (1). |
| Hoard | Trewhiddle (1774) 114 Saxon Dep. 871 – 5. |

Cumberland

| Hoard | Beaumont (1884) 2090 Longcross Dep. 1360. |

Derbyshire

Mint	Derby **S** Aethelstan – Edward C. (13), **N** William I – II (4), Henry I (1), Stephen (1).
Hoard	Derby (Sept. 1937) 634 Edward I – III.
	Sheldon (1867) 95 Henry I – Stephen.
Museum	Derby Museum, Tutbury Hoard, Saxon coins of Derby mint.
Society	Derbyshire N.S. (Derby).

Devon

| Mints | Barnstaple **S** Aethelred II – Edward C. (9), **N** William I – II (1), Henry I (1). |
| | Exeter **S** Alfred – Harold II (57), **N** William I – II |

(11), Henry I (3), Stephen (3). Tealby (4), Short-
cross (8), Longcross (4), Edward II.
Civil War Exeter (Sept. 1643 – 46).
Recoinage of William III (1695 – 1697).
Lydford S Edward the Martyr – Edward C. (11).
Totnes S Aethelred II – Canute (15), N William I –
II (2), Henry I (1).

Societies   Devon and Exeter N.S.; North Devon N.S. (Barn-
staple); Plymouth N.S.

Dorset

Mints   Dorchester S Aethelstan – Edward C. (7), N
William I – II (4), Henry I (2).
Shaftesbury S Aethelstan – Harold II (20), N
William I – II (7), Henry I (4), Stephen (2).
Sherborne N Henry of Anjou (Stephen).
Wareham S Aethelstan – Harold II (11), N William
I – II (5), Henry I (5), Matilda.
Weymouth, Civil War (Aug. 1643 – June 1644).

Museums   Dorchester County Museum. Roman.
Pitt Rivers Museum, Farnham, Blandford. Roman
collection of General Pitt-Rivers.

Durham

Mint   Durham N William I – II (2), Henry I (1), Stephen
(2), Tealby (3), Shortcross (3), Longcross (3),
Edward I – III and late mediaeval.
Tudor Henry VII – VIII.

Hoard   Durham 2 (May 1930) 572 coins of Edward I – III.
Dep. 1360.

Museums   Darlington Museum Pence of Durham mint.
Cathedral Library, Durham Great Lumley Treasure
Trove (Elizabeth I).
Southshields Library and Museum. Roman.

Society   **Tyneside N.S.**

Essex

Mints   Colchester S Aethelred II – Harold II (24), N
William I – II (12), Henry I (4), Stephen (1), Tealby
(3).
Civil War (June – Aug. 1648).
Siege pieces Ten shillings in gold.
Horndon S A few coins of Edward C. A brief mint.
Maldon S Aethelstan – Harold II (14), N William
I – II (4).

Hoard   Colchester (July 1902) 10,926 shortcross Dep. 1260.
One of the largest mediaeval hoards ever recorded.

Society   Chelmsford and District N.S.

Gloucestershire

Mints   Berkeley **S** Edward C. only 3 coins known.

Bristol **S** Aethelred II – Edward C. (14), **N** William I – II (8), Henry I (9), Stephen (2), Tealby (3), Longcross, Edward I.
Tudor Henry VIII, Edward VI.
Civil War (1643 – 45) B.R. monogram.
Recoinage of William III (1695 – 97).

Gloucester **S** Alfred – Harold II (20), **N** William I – II (9), Henry I (7), Stephen (5), Tealby (4), Longcross (4).

Winchcombe **S** Edgar – Harold II (7), **N** William I – II (1).

Museums   City Museum, Bristol. Roman, Bristol Mint.
City Museum, Gloucester. Anglo Saxon, Roman, and mediaeval.

Society   Cheltenham N.S.

Hampshire

Mints   Southampton **S** Edgar – Harold II, **N** William I – II (3), Henry I (3), Stephen.
Winchester **S** Egbert – Harold II (75), **N** William I – II (14), Henry I (17), Stephen (8), Tealby (4), Shortcross (16), Longcross (4).

Hoards   Awbridge (1902) 180 Stephen, 9 Tealby.
Beaworth (June 1833) 8,000 – 12,000 William I – II. Dep. 1087.
Crondall (1828) 100 gold. Dep. 670.

Museums   Tudor House Museum, Southampton. Roman.
City Museum, Winchester. Roman; Winchester mint.

Societies   Southampton and District N.S.; Winchester N.S.; Wessex N.S. (Bournemouth).

Herefordshire

Mint   Hereford **S** Aethelstan – Harold II, **N** William I – II (11), Henry I (5), Stephen (4), Tealby (4), Longcross (4).

Museum   Hereford. Roman including the Llangarron Hoard, English.

Hertfordshire

Mint   Hertford **S** Aethelstan – Edward C. (17), **N** William I – II (3).

Hoard   Watford No. 1. (1818) 1127 William I, Henry I, Stephen. Dep. 1140.

Museum   Letchworth Museum and Art Gallery. Miscellaneous.

Huntingdonshire

Mint	Huntingdon **S** Edwig – Harold II (28), **N** William I – II (4), Henry I (1), Stephen (1).

Kent

Mints	Canterbury **S** Egbert – Harold II (35), **N** William I – II (17), Henry I (12), Stephen (8), Tealby (9), Shortcross (31), Longcross (9), Edward I – IV. Tudor Henry VII, Edward VI. Dover **S** Edgar – Harold II (22), **N** William I – II (7), Henry I (2), Stephen (1). Hythe **S** Edward C. (3), **N** William I – II (1). Rochester **S** Aethelstan – Harold II (19), **N** William I – II (6), Henry I (2), Shortcross (3). Romney **S** Aethelred II – Harold II (15), **N** William I – II (5), Henry I (2). Sandwich **S** Aethelred II – Edward C. (4), **N** William I – II (5), Henry I (5), Stephen (2).
Hoards	Gravesend (1838) 540 Anglo Saxon pence. Dep. 875. Maidstone (1952) Mediaeval English.
Museum	Maidstone Museum and Art Gallery. Roman, Saxon and Norman pence of Kent mints.
Societies	Kent N.S. (Maidstone); Medway Towns N.S. Rochester.

Lancashire

Hoards	Cuerdale (May 1840) 7,000 Saxon and Viking. Dep. 890. Eccles (1864) 6,000 shortcross. Dep. 1240 – 1. Halton Moor (Feb. 1815) 860 Canute. Dep. 1025.
Museums	Blackburn Museum. Hart Collection (Comprehensive collection of many series). Lancaster Museum. Roman and English.
Societies	Lancs. and Cheshire N.S. (Manchester); Preston and District N.S.; Merseyside N.S. (Liverpool).

Leicestershire

Mint	Leicester **S** Edgar – Harold II (21), **N** William I – II (5), Henry I (6), Stephen (1), Tealby (2).
Hoards	Leicester (Jan. 1927) 227 Tealby. Dep. 1180.
Museum	Leicester City Museum and Art Gallery. Comprehensive collection of all periods. Leicester mint.
Society	Leicester and District N.S.

Lincolnshire

Mints	Horncastle **S** Aethelred II. Lincoln **S** Aethelred I – Harold II (94), **N** William I – II (22), Henry I (3), Stephen (11), Tealby (6), Shortcross (16), Longcross (4), Edward I.

	Stamford **S** Edgar – Harold II (52), **N** William I – II (10), Henry I (6), Stephen (2).
Hoards	Stamford No. 2 (22nd Oct. 1866) 3,000 English and Scottish Groats. Dep. 1465.
	Tealby 5,700 Tealby pennies of Henry II. Dep. 1170 – 80.
	Tetney (May 1945) 394 Anglo Saxon and Danish pennies. Dep. 970.
Museum	City and County Museum, Lincoln. Roman and Saxon.
Societies	Lincs. N.S. (Grimsby); Horncastle N.S.

London

Mints	London Roman (4th Century A.D.) **S** Throughout the period (141), **N** William I – II (35), Henry I (37), Stephen (23), Tealby (18), Shortcross (44), Longcross (11), Edward I – II and throughout mediaeval period.
	Tower Mint 1300 – 1811.
	Durham House, Strand. Tudor (Dec. 1548 – Oct. 1549).
	London Mint, Tower Hill 1813 – Present day.
Hoards	Several important hoards have been found in London, details of which may be found in J. D. Thompson's *Inventory of Coin Hoards*.
Museum	Coin Room, British Museum — The National Collection.
Societies	Royal N.S.; British N.S.; London N.S.

Middlesex

Hoard	Hounslow (1861) 378 groats of Henry VI – Richard III. Dep. 1495 – 1500.
Society	Hayes (Middlesex) and District Coin Club.

Norfolk

Mints	Caistor **S** Canute Brief mint only.
	King's Lynn **N** Shortcross (3).
	Norwich **S** Aethelstan – Harold II (38), **N** William I – II (15), Henry I (14), Stephen (18), Tealby (8), Shortcross (4), Longcross (4).
	Mediaeval Edward IV (Norwich ryal and groat).
	Thetford **S** Aethelred II – Harold II (48), **N** William I – II (13), Henry I (16), Stephen (4), Tealby (4).

Northamptonshire

Mints	Northampton **S** Edgar – Harold II, **N** William I – II (4), Henry I (7), Stephen, Tealby (7), Shortcross (10), Longcross (4).

| | Peterborough **S** Edgar, **N** William I – II (1). |
| Society | Peterborough and District N.S. |

Northumberland

Mints	Corbridge **N** Stephen (irregular issue).
	Newcastle upon Tyne **N** Stephen, Tealby (1), Longcross (4), Edward I.
Hoards	Hensleyside (1854) 257 Edward I – II pence. Dep. 1300 – 20.
	Hexham (1833) 8,000 stycas of the Kings of Northumberland and the Archbishop of York.
Museums	Chesters Museum, Hexham. Roman including **Carrawburgh.**
	Blackgate Museum, Newcastle upon Tyne. Roman.
Society	Tyneside N.S. (Newcastle).

Nottinghamshire

Mints	Newark **S** Aethelred II, **N** Stephen.
	Civil War (Newark surrendered 6th May 1646). Siege pieces — half crown, shilling, ninepence, sixpence.
	Nottingham **S** Aethelstan – Harold II (13), **N** William I – II (5), Henry I (1), Stephen (1).
Hoard	Fishpool (March 22nd 1966) 1,237 gold nobles of Edward III and Edward IV. Largest hoard of mediaeval gold in England.
Museums	Newark on Trent Municipal Museum — Siege pieces.
	City Museum and Art Gallery, Nottingham. **Roman.**
Societies	The Numismatic Society of Notts. (Nottingham); Worksop and District N.S.

Oxfordshire

Mint	Oxford **S** Alfred – Harold II (29), **N** William I – II (9), Henry I (4), Stephen (3), Tealby (3), Shortcross (10), Longcross (4).
	Civil War (Jan. 1643 – June 1646).
Hoard	Oxford No. 2 (1868) 213 coins Edward I – III. Dep. 1351.
Museum	Heberden Coin Room, Ashmolean Museum, Oxford. Large collection of all periods.
Society	Oxford N.S.

Shropshire

| Mint | Shrewsbury **S** Aethelstan – Harold II (29), **N** William I – II (7), Henry I (1), Stephen (2), Tealby (1), Shortcross (2), Longcross (2). |

	Civil War (Oct. – Dec. 1642).
Museum	Shrewsbury Museum. Roman, Shrewsbury mint.

Somerset

Mints	Axbridge S Aethelred II – Canute.
	Bath S Edward the Elder – Edward C., N William I – II (4), Henry I (1).
	Bridport S Aethelred II – Edward C. (4), N William I – II (3).
	Bruton S Aethelred II, Canute. Few coins known.
	Cadbury S Aethelred II – Canute. Brief mint.
	Crewkerne S Aethelred II, Canute.
	Ilchester S Aethelred II – Harold II (22), N William I – II (4), Henry I (1), Stephen (1), Tealby (3), Longcross (4).
	Langport S Aethelstan – Edward C. (6).
	Taunton S Aethelred II – Harold II (6), N William I – II (2), Henry I (1), Stephen (1).
	Watchet S Aethelred II – Edward C. (4), N William I – II (1), Stephen (2).
Museums	Somerset County Museum, Taunton. Roman.
	Wells Museum. Miscellaneous.
Society	Bath and Bristol N.S.

Staffordshire

Mints	Stafford S Aethelstan – Edward C. (7), N William I – II (4), Stephen (1), Tealby (2).
	Tamworth S Aethelstan – Edward C. (9), N William I – II (2), Henry I (2), Stephen (1).
Hoards	Tamworth (1877) 300 pence of William I – II. Dep. 1090.
	Tutbury (June 1831) 20,000 shortcross and pence of Edward I – II.
Museums	Stoke on Trent Museum and Art Gallery. Tutbury Hoard, Lightwood Hoard (Roman).
	Castle Museum, Tamworth. Tamworth mint.
Society	Walsall N.S.

Suffolk

Mints	Bury St. Edmunds S Harold I, Edward C., N William I – II (1), Henry I, Stephen (3), Tealby, Shortcross (6), Longcross (6), Edward I – III.
	Ipswich S Edgar – Harold II (28), N William I – II (9), Henry I (6), Stephen (6), Tealby (3), Shortcross (2).
	Sudbury S Aethelred II – Edward C. (16), N William I – II (2), Henry I (2), Stephen (2).

Hoard	Ipswich (Oct. 1863) 500 Aethelred II. Dep. 979.
Museum	Moyes Hall Museum, Bury St. Edmunds. Miscellaneous.
Society	Ipswich N.S.

Surrey

Mints	Guildford **S** Aethelred II – Harold II (10), **N** William I – II (2).
	Southwark **S** Aethelred II – Edward C. (28), **N** William I – II (10), Henry I (5), Stephen (4).
	Tudor (Suffolk Palace) Edward VI.
Hoard	Dorking (1817) 974 Saxon pence. Dep. 865 – 6.
Societies	Surrey N.S. (Croydon); Kingston N.S.

Sussex

Mints	Chichester **S** Aethelstan – Harold II (17), **N** William I – II (3), Henry I (2), Stephen (1), Shortcross (4).
	Hastings **S** Aethelred II – Harold II (13), **N** William I – II (7), Henry I (5), Stephen (4).
	Lewis **S** Aethelstan – Harold II (30), **N** William I – II (5), Henry I (5), Stephen (5), Tealby (1).
	Steyning **S** Canute – Harold II (5), **N** William I – II (3).
	Pevensey **N** William I – II (1), Henry I (1), Stephen (2).
	Rye **N** Stephen (1).
Hoards	Balcombe (May 1897) 730 Edward I – II. Dep. 1380.
	Chancton (Dec. 1866) 1,720 Edward C.
Museums	Hastings Museum. Anglo Saxon and Norman pennies of Sussex mints.
	Hove Museum of Art. Miscellaneous.
Societies	Rye Coin Club; Worthing and District N.S.

Warwickshire

Mints	Warwick **S** Edward the Martyr – Harold II (18), **N** William I – II (8), Henry I (4), Stephen (4).
	Soho, Birmingham. Copper coinage 1797 – 1807 including "Cartwheel" issue of 1797/8.
	Heaton, Birmingham. Bronze coins 1874 –6, 1881 –2, 1912, 1918 – 19.
	Kings Norton, Birmingham. Bronze pennies 1918 – 19.
Museum	Birmingham Museum. Comprehensive collection.
Societies	Birmingham N.S.; Coventry and District N.S.

Wiltshire

| Mints | Bedwyn **S** Edward C. (1), **N** William I – II (1). |
| | Cricklade **S** Aethelred II – Edward C. (16), **N** |

	William I – II (4).
	Malmesbury **S** Edgar – Harold II (10), **N** William I – II (3).
	Salisbury **S** Aethelred II – Edward C. (14), **N** William I – II (5), Henry I (3), Stephen (1), Tealby (2).
	Warminster **S** Aethelred II – Edward C. (6).
	Wilton **S** Edgar – Harold II (25), **N** William I – II (5), Henry I (3), Stephen (4), Tealby (3), Shortcross (2), Longcross (4).
Hoard	Boyton (July 1935) 4,147 Longcross.
Museums	Devizes Museum. Roman.
	Salisbury and S. Wiltshire Museum. Miscellaneous.
Society	Swindon and District N.S.

Worcestershire

Mints	Pershore **S** Edward C.
	Worcester **S** Aethelred II – Harold II (24), **N** William I – II (10), Henry I (3), Stephen (5), Tealby (1), Shortcross (4).
	Civil War (1646) Half crown.
Hoard	Worcester (1850) 240 Tealby.
Society	West Midland N.S. (Dudley).

Yorkshire

Mints	York **S** Kings of Northumbria – Harold II (93), **N** William I – II (12), Henry I (7), Stephen (5), Tealby (8), Shortcross (14), Longcross (5).
	Mint of King York Castle.
	Mint of Archbishop York Palace.
	Edward I – III, Henry IV – VI.
	Tudor.
	Civil War (surrendered to parliament) 1644.
	Recoinage of William III (1695).
	Kingston upon Hull. Mediaeval Edward I.
	Pontefract. Civil War (June 1648 – March 1654). Siege pieces.
Hoards	Scotton (June 1924) 310 Edward I – II. Dep. 1324.
	Skipton (July 1949) 372 Edward III. Dep. 1399.
	York No. 2. Bootham (Sept. 1953) 904 longcross.
Museums	Tolson Memorial Museum, Huddersfield. Miscellaneous.
	City Museum, Leeds. Roman, Saxon, Norman, York Mint.
	Yorks Museum, York. Comprehensive collection.
Societies	Yorks N.S. (Leeds, etc.); Huddersfield N.S.; Sheffield and District N.S.; Hull N.S.